Love to Sew

Children's Sun Hats

Dedication

This book is dedicated to the memory of Michael Rees,
my wonderful Dad.

Love to Sew

Children's Sun Hats

Gill Stratton

Search Press

First published in Great Britain 2012

Search Press Limited
Wellwood, North Farm Road,
Tunbridge Wells, Kent TN2 3DR

Text copyright © Gill Stratton 2013

Photographs by Paul Bricknell

Photographs and design copyright © Search Press Ltd. 2013

ISBN: 978-1-84448-836-0

The Publishers and author can accept no responsibility for any consequences arising from the information, advice or instructions given in this publication.

Suppliers
If you have difficulty in obtaining any of the materials and equipment mentioned in this book, then please visit the Search Press website for details of suppliers: www.searchpress.com

You are invited to visit the author's website:
www.elizabethreesmillinery.com

Acknowledgements

Huge thanks to my wonderful husband, Neil, and children, Lucy, William and Daniel for all their enthusiasm, patience, love and support. Thank you to my fantastic Mum, Marian Rees, for her determination to teach me to sew (I got there in the end), her encouragement and belief in me. Thank you to all my family and friends for their support, especially Bob and Jean Stratton.
To Jane Cave at Mille Fleurs (the best hat shop in the UK) for giving me the opportunity and training to realise my dream of becoming a milliner. To Inger Arthur who initiated this journey, and to Roz Dace for asking me to write this book. To Sophie Kersey for helping me along with her expert guidance and editorial support – I have enjoyed every minute. To all at Search Press and Paul Bricknell – thank you. And lastly, thank you to all my beautiful hat models: Lucy, William and Daniel Stratton, Samuel Burgess, Ben, Sammy and Tom Gannon, Emma Boulcott, Alex and Eleanor Lee, Ruby Eves, Eddie and Flo Warwick – the book looks so great because of you.

Printed in China

Whale Hat, page 20

Bow Hat, page 22

Animal Hat, page 28

Bicycle Hat, page 30

Reversible Hat, page 36

Legionnaire's Hat, page 38

Floppy Brim, page 48

Strawberry Hat, page 50

White Hat, page 24

Contents

Train Hat, page 26

Sun Visor, page 32

Pirate Bandana, page 34

Traditional Hat, page 40

Bird Hat, page 42

Patchwork Hat, page 44

Girl's Sun Visor, page 46

Daisy Hat, page 52

Explorer's Hat, page 54

Denim Hat, page 56

Dress Hat, page 58

Introduction

Sun hats have become a summer essential to keep the sun from children's delicate faces. However if, like me, you spend most of the summer nagging your children to put their hats on, then this book is for you. I found that if I let my children choose the shape and colour of the hat, they were much more likely to wear it. It is also great fun to involve your child in the creation of the hat; they have some great ideas, and by using their favourite hobby or animal as inspiration, you make it their own personal hat which they will wear with pride.

There are so many different fabrics for children, and online you will find a vast array of cotton and linen fabrics, funky novelty buttons and beautiful ribbons. I hope you will find plenty of inspiration in this book, but that you will also add your own ideas, so that each hat will be truly unique to your child in both fit and style.

There are twenty projects with hats for lots of different occasions: from a sun visor which will squash easily into a handbag for holidays to a girl's floppy-brimmed sun hat that would look beautiful for a wedding or special occasion. There are hats for babies which would make a lovely handmade present for a new arrival. I have also included a bandana style hat and caps that may appeal more to boys – especially slightly older boys.

We throw away so many clothes, so I have included a section on making recycled hats. A pair of battered old jeans can make a fabulous sun hat. Even an old dress from the bottom of the wardrobe could become your next sun hat project. It's very easy to get hooked!

At the beginning of the book are the basic techniques you will use when putting a hat together, such as creating a traditional brim and crown, a peak brim, and a sectioned crown. There are pictures and explanations showing you each step of the way. Each project has further instructions on how to finish the hat and create a great trim, so even those new to sewing will soon be producing a sun hat their child will be desperate to wear!

General guide to children's head sizes:

0–12 months: 43.2–49.5cm (17–19½in)
12–24 months: 49.5–52.8cm (19½–20¾in)
2–4 years: 52.8–54.6cm (20¾–21½in)
4–8 years: 54.6–56cm (21½–22in)

Materials & equipment

No specialist millinery equipment is needed to make the hats. All the materials used are available at any good fabric or craft store, or online. You do not even have to buy new fabrics – you could use old shirts or blouses that were heading for the bin. There are no rules for what you can and can't use for hat trims – even upholstery tassels could make a fun trim, or just a few old buttons.

Fabrics

Any type of fabric can be used, from light cotton to heavier soft furnishing fabrics. The weight of the fabric will determine whether or not you need to use interfacing. Some of the heavier cottons and linens hold their shape well and will not need interfacing. I source many of the fabrics online and I love using Japanese cotton fabric – you will find some beautiful and fun prints. I also love to mix and match; having different fabrics for the brim and crown will make the hat more eye-catching. Never throw your scraps of fabric away – they can all be used to make a flower or a pocket to trim the hat.

Threads

I have used standard cotton sewing thread. I tend to stick to white cotton, especially when using a mix of fabrics and colours. I like to see the top stitching on the hat, as I feel this gives it a more professional finish.

Opposite
A variety of fabrics suitable for making hats that children will love.

Sewing machine

A basic sewing machine is all you need to start making a hat. I have used a straight line stitch in all the projects. If your machine has a back stitch function, this would be advisable for finishing off the beginning and end of each stitch line. The tension on your machine will need to be adjusted to the fabric you are using.

Embellishments

There are countless ways to trim a hat and all trims shown in this book are interchangeable between hat shapes. I have used different types of ribbons for trims such as silk, grosgrain and patterned ribbon; you can even use bias binding.

Buttons are also a really easy way of giving a hat some interest, and you can make your own covered buttons using scraps of fabric or raid your old button box. You can also find a vast array of fun novelty buttons online, such as spotty or candy-striped (you can even get cupcake or dinosaur-shaped buttons).

Beads have also been used in the trimming. These can be bought very cheaply, but never throw away an old bead necklace, as you can use the beads for your hats.

Always keep the scraps of fabric after cutting out your hat, as these can be used to make fabric flowers, bows or pockets.

Other materials

You will need some baking parchment to make hat patterns from the templates shown from page 60 onwards. Depending on the weight of the fabric, you will need some medium-weight iron-on interfacing. I use the iron-on variety rather than sew-on, as it makes life easier if you need to trim or make an adjustment. For the peak brims, I have used the heaviest weight stiff interfacing so that the peak holds its shape. Other materials used in the making of some of the hats include snap fasteners, 1cm (³/₈in) wide elastic, 2cm (¾in) wide hook and loop tape and buttons for self covering, all available from fabric or craft stores.

You will also need a sharp pair of fabric scissors for cutting your patterns, embroidery scissors for undoing stitches and trimming loose threads, a tape measure for measuring your child's head, and dressmaking pins and needles. A stitch ripper and thimble may also come in handy.

An iron is of course required for the iron-on interfacing, and for pressing the hats at various stages.

Basic techniques

Once you have mastered these basic techniques, you can make any hat. All the templates for the hats can be found on pages 60–64 and traced or photocopied, then enlarged to the required hat size.

Using patterns to cut out the fabric

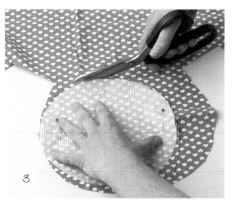

Measuring your child's head

For a general guide to children's head sizes at various ages, see the table on page 6. However, if you are able to measure the child's head, this is how:

1 Hold a tape measure around your child's head. The tape measure should sit just above their ears and eyebrows. Insert a finger between the head and tape to ensure that the hat will not be too tight and will leave a little room for growth.

2 Use the template on page 62 to make a paper pattern for the brim. Fold the fabric over to allow for the required size of the brim, and align one edge of the pattern along the fold.

3 To minimise fabric waste, once you have cut out the brim, open out the fabric and use this section to cut out your crown (see the template on page 60). Repeat this process, so that you will have two brims and two crowns.

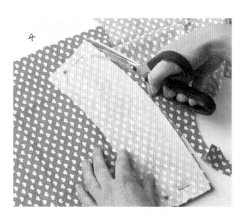

4 Place the paper pattern for the middle section (see page 60) against the fold as for the brim. Pin and cut it out. Repeat so that you have two middle sections.

The fabric pieces cut out. You will have two crowns, two middle sections and two brims. These do not need to be all the same fabric; you may choose to have one crown and one middle section in a different fabric, as this will become the lining inside the hat.

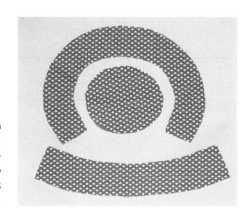

Using iron-on interfacing

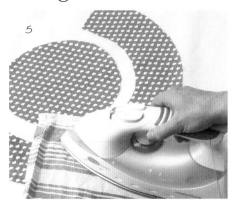

5 Place the interfacing on the work surface (fusible side up) and put one brim section, one middle section and one crown right side up on top. Unless your fabric is very thin, you will not need to use interfacing on all pieces. Place a clean, damp tea towel over the area you are going to iron, and press with the iron to attach the interfacing to the fabric pieces. Cut out these pieces.

Assembling a brim

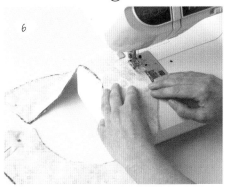

6 Thread the machine with your chosen thread. Take the two brim pieces, one with interfacing and one without. Pin them together, right sides together. Stitch along the outer curved edge with a 5mm (¼in) seam. Open out and press the seams to one side.

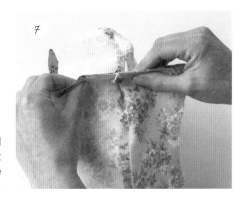

7 Take the ends of the brim piece and join them together to create a circle, right sides together. Ensure that the middle seams match and pin the ends together.

8 Machine stitch along the pinned ends with a 5mm (¼in) seam.

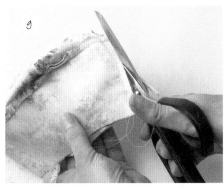

9 Trim back the seam so that it is not too bulky, and press open.

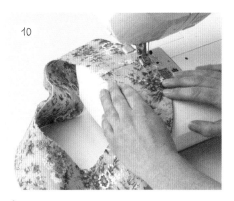

10 Turn the brim right side out and press to give a sharp edge. Top stitch along the brim 5mm (¼in) from the edge.

Attaching the crown to the middle section

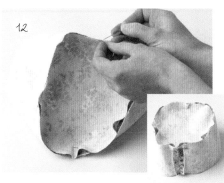

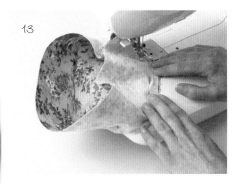

11 Take the middle section and place right sides together. Sew along the ends with a 5mm (¼in) seam, and press the seam open.

12 Pin the crown to the middle section, right sides together. First pin the front, back and middle, then add pins in between if needed.

13 Sew these pieces together with a 5mm (¼in) seam.

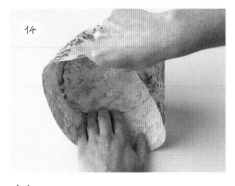

14 Turn the crown right side out. Finger press the seams downwards.

15 Take the base off the sewing machine to show the arm, and top stitch the seam down 5mm (¼in) from the edge.

16 Finish off the crown by top stitching 5mm (¼in) either side of the middle section seam.

Attaching the brim to the crown

17 Place the brim round the middle section, matching the back seams together, and pin together. First pin the front, back and middle and then add pins in between.

18 Sew together using a 5mm (¼in) seam.

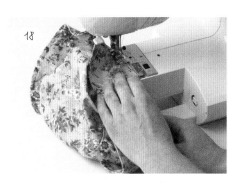

Making and attaching the lining

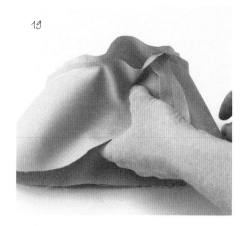

19 Sew the crown and middle section of the lining together in the same way as for the main hat, but when attaching the crown, leave a 10cm (4in) hole for pulling through.

20 With the lining section inside out, turn the brim back on the hat and place this inside the lining section. Make sure the back seams are together. Pin in place.

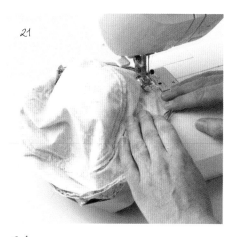

21 Turn this piece hat side out, and machine sew together. Sew just above the sewing line where you attached the brim.

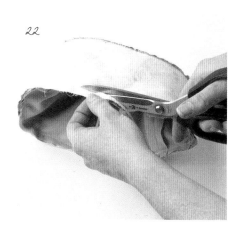

22 Trim back the seam to avoid it getting too bulky.

23 Pull the hat back through the hole in the lining.

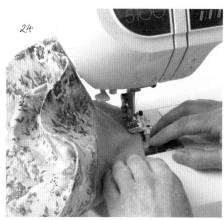

24 Machine sew the hole together, and press the hat.

25

26

The finished hat, inside and out.

$\mathit{25}$ Sew a 5mm (¼in) top stitch either side of the back seam on the brim.

$\mathit{26}$ Finish the hat by top stitching 5mm (¼in) around the middle seam of the hat which joins the brim to the crown. This will also help to hold the lining in place.

Making a six-part crown

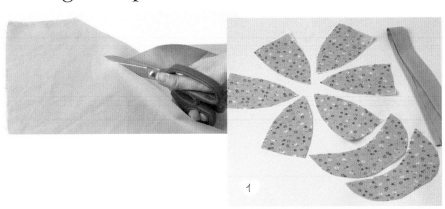

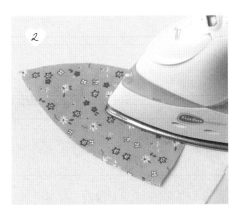

2

1

$\mathit{1}$ Cut out six crown triangles for the hat and six for the lining, using the template on page 61. Cut out two peak pieces using the template on page 60. Cut out a head ribbon, using the same fabric as the lining. The head ribbon should be cut on the cross (at a 45° angle – see inset) to make a bias strip 6cm (2½in) wide and 1cm (³⁄₈in) longer than the head measurement to which you are making the hat.

$\mathit{2}$ Place the interfacing on the work surface (fusible side up) and put six triangles right side up on top. Place a clean damp tea towel over the area you are going to iron, and press with the iron to attach the interfacing to the fabric pieces. Cut out these pieces.

3 Draw round the peak pattern from page 60 on heavyweight interfacing and cut out.

4 Take two of the crown triangles and place them right sides together. Machine sew down one side of the triangles using a 5mm (¼in) seam. Attach a third triangle piece in the same way.

5 Repeat with the other three triangles. Press each section with the seams facing to one side. Take the two sections and pin them together so that the tops of the triangles match.

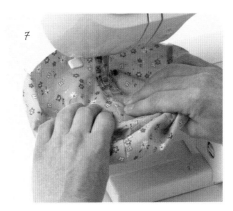

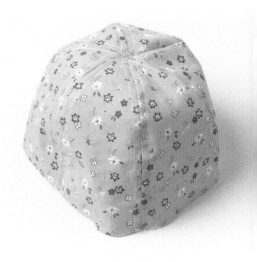

6 Sew these sections together, starting at the bottom and continuing over the top and down the other side. It can be tricky to get the triangles to match perfectly. If they are uneven, you could add a button on top when the hat is finished to help disguise this.

7 Remove the base of the sewing machine to reveal the arm. Turn the hat right side out and top stitch 5mm (¼in) either side of each seam. Go straight over the top and down the other side of the hat to give a continuous stitch line. Try to create a star shape on top of the hat. Repeat the above process for the lining of the hat; however you do not need to add the top stitching at the end.

The finished crown.

Making and attaching a peak

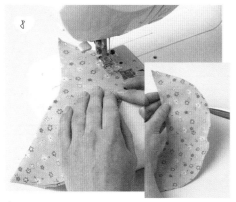

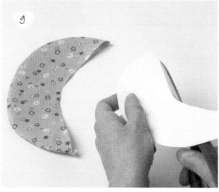

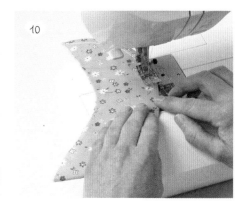

8 Place the peak pieces right sides together and pin. Sew along the outer curved edge using a 5mm (¼in) seam. Snip little triangle shapes along this edge towards the seam, but do not cut through it. Turn right side out and press to give a sharp edge.

9 Trim the heavyweight interfacing so that it fits neatly inside the peak. The inner curve should be 1cm (³⁄₈in) shallower than the fabric.

10 Press the peak with the interfacing inside and top stitch 5mm (¼in) from the outer edge.

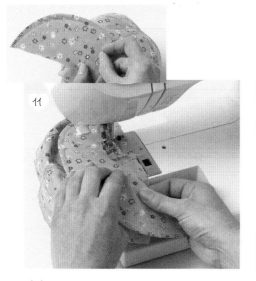

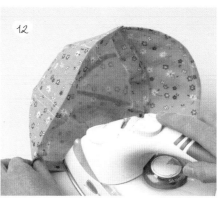

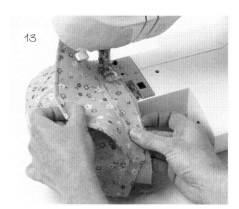

11 Place a pin to mark the centre point of the peak and crown. Match these points together and pin the peak to the crown so that the peak is facing up towards the top of the crown. Sew the peak to the crown, approximately 2.5cm (1in) from the bottom, as close to the interfacing in the peak as possible.

12 Turn the bottom of the crown 2.5cm (1in) under and press well.

13 Put the lining inside the hat right side out, matching the triangles, and sew to the hat underneath the line that has just been pressed.

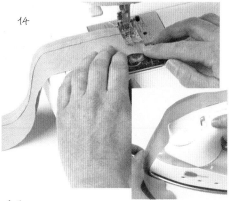

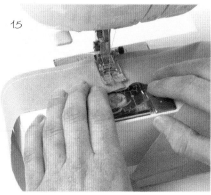

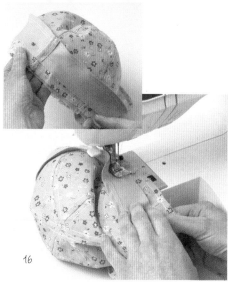

14 Take the head ribbon and edge one side by pressing down 1cm (³/₈in) and stitching along the length. Use the iron to curve the head ribbon to a head shape. Hold one section down with the iron and pull the head ribbon down and through, underneath the iron.

15 Join the ends of the head ribbon together using a 5mm (¼in) seam.

16 Check that the head ribbon fits and pin the unfinished edge, with the seams showing, along the pressed line. Make sure the back seams are together. Sew the ribbon in place. The aim is to hide all the stitching with the head ribbon, so make sure the stitch line for the head ribbon is just above the line where the peak is stitched to the crown.

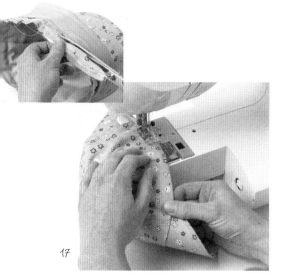

17 Trim any excess fabric away below the ribbon. Fold the head ribbon back and press well. Finally top stitch 5mm (¼in) from the bottom of the hat all around to help keep the ribbon in place and give a professional finish.

The finished peaked cap.

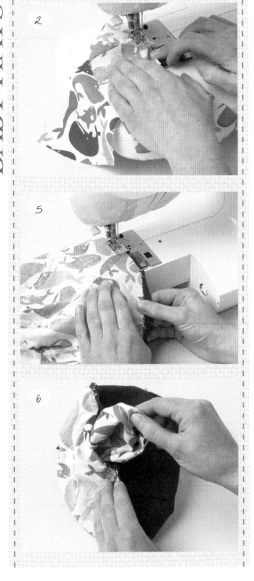

Whale Hat

Materials

- lightweight interfacing
- whale fabric, 46 x 56cm (18 x 22in) for the main hat
- dark blue fabric, 46 x 56cm (18 x 22in) for the lining
- thread

Tools

- fabric scissors
- iron
- pins
- sewing machine

1 Use the crown section template on page 60 to cut out six sections in the main hat fabric. Turn the pattern over and cut six sections in the lining material. The lining sections and the main hat sections should be the opposite of each other. Follow the instructions on page 13 for using the iron-on interfacing on the six sections of the main hat.

2 Place two sections of the main hat fabric right sides together. Take the top right-hand sides of the sections and sew down the right-hand side. These two pieces do not naturally feel like they fit together, so hold them together as you sew from top to bottom. Continue adding each piece until you have a hat shape.

3 Press the seams to one side. Remove the base from the sewing machine to reveal the arm. Turn the hat right side out and sew 5mm (¼in) either side of each seam, continuing over the top and down the hat to create one stitch line. Try to create a star shape on the top of the hat.

4 Repeat the process for the lining, but there is no need to overstitch the seams.

5 Turn each hat inside out, and place right sides together. Make sure that the seams are matching and stitch 5mm (¼in) from the bottom of the hat, but leave a 5cm (2in) gap.

6 Pull the hat back through the hole, so that it is the correct way around and press the hat. Stitch along the bottom of the hat, as close as possible to the bottom to secure the hole. Add another top stitch line slightly above the first line.

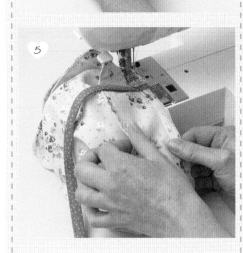

Bow Hat

Materials

- lightweight interfacing
- flower fabric, ½ metre (½ yard) to make 1 crown piece, 1 middle section and 2 wavy brims
- spotty fabric, ½ metre (½ yard) to make 1 crown piece and 1 middle section for the lining and bias strips for 2 chin ties and 1 bow trim
- thread
- button

Tools

- fabric scissors
- iron
- pins
- sewing machine
- needle

1 Cut out the pieces as described, using the templates on page 61 and 62. Follow the instructions on page 13 for using the iron-on interfacing on one brim piece, the floral middle section and crown. Follow the instructions on page 14 for attaching the crown to the middle section.

2 Take the two wavy brim sections and place right sides together. This brim crosses over at the back of the hat. Stitch using a 5mm (¼in) seam from the sides of the brim and along following the scallops as closely as possible. Snip small triangles into the curved edges of the brim; be careful not to cut the stitching. Turn the brim right side out and press well. Overstitch 5mm (¼in) along the edge of the brim, following the scallops.

3 Take the crown and pin the end of the brim to the back seam of the crown. Pin all round until the brim crosses over at the back. Remove the base from the sewing machine to reveal the arm and stitch the brim to the crown using a 5mm (¼in) seam.

4 Take the fabric for the chin ties and fold over on the cross at a 45° angle. Use the sewing machine to stitch 1cm (³⁄₈in) along the cross to create a bias strip. Cut this from the fabric to create a tube (rouleau).Thread a needle with thread and sew a securing stitch into the top side of the tube. Push the blunt end of the needle though the tube and gradually push through until you pull the whole tube right the way through. Press the tube and cut to create two lengths 30.5cm (12in) long. Take one end of each length and neatly push the end back up inside the hole and press, then stitch in place.

5 Find the middle of each side of the hat and pin. Flip the brim up and stitch the unfinished ends of the ties to the hat, sewing below the stitch line where the brim is attached to the crown.

6 Follow the instructions on page 15 for making and attaching the lining. Ensure that the ties are on the right side of the lining.

7 For the trim, make another rouleau, finishing off both ends. Tie into a small bow and secure with a pretty button.

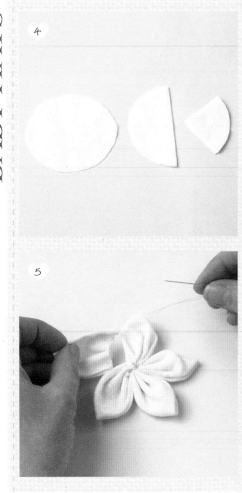

White Hat

Materials

- white fabric, ½ metre (½ yard) to make 6 triangles for the crown and 2 brims for the hat and 6 triangles for the lining
- white fabric, 25 x 40cm (10 x 15¾in) for the flower trim
- lightweight interfacing
- button
- thread

Tools

- fabric scissors
- iron
- pins
- sewing machine
- needle

1 Take the crown triangle template on page 64 and cut twelve triangles to create the crown and lining. Using the instructions on page 12, cut two brim shapes using the brim template on page 62.

2 Iron on the interfacing using the instructions on page 13 to one brim piece and six triangles.

3 Assemble the crown of the hat using the instructions on page 16 for making a six-part crown. Follow the instructions on page 13 for assembling the brim, and then the instructions for attaching the brim to the crown on page 14. For the lining, follow the same instructions for putting together a six-part crown, but leave a 10cm (4in) gap for pulling the hat through. Make sure that the gap is left in the middle so that the top and bottom of the section is secure. Follow the instructions for attaching the lining on pages 15 and 16, from step 20.

4 Cut five circles of white fabric 10cm (4in) in diameter. Press the circles and fold them in half and then into quarters, pressing at each stage.

5 Thread a needle and, taking one of the quarters, sew a running stitch along the curved edge. Gather this section together to form a petal shape. Continue by adding each petal in the same way. Once you have attached the five petals, pull into a flower shape and secure with a couple of back stitches.

6 Choose a pretty button and stitch it to the middle of the flower and then stitch the flower trim to the side of the hat.

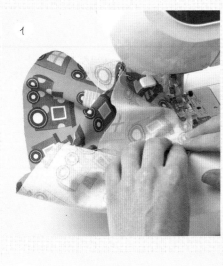

Train Hat

Materials

- lightweight interfacing
- heavyweight non-iron stiff interfacing for the peak
- train fabric, 70cm (27½in) wide x 40cm (15¾in) high to make 1 crown and 1 middle section
- spotty fabric, ½ metre (½ yard) to make 1 crown and 1 middle section for the lining, 2 peaks and 1 head ribbon
- 2 buttons
- thread

Tools

- fabric scissors
- pins
- sewing machine
- needle
- iron

1 Use the template on page 60 to cut one crown in the train fabric, and the template on page 61 to cut one middle section in the train fabric. Follow the instructions on page 13 for using the iron-on interfacing and iron to the train middle section and crown. Use the instructions on page 14 for attaching the crown to the middle section.

2 Using the spotty fabric, cut one crown and middle section and again repeat the method of attaching the crown to the middle section.

3 Cut out a head ribbon from the spotty fabric. The head ribbon should be cut on the cross (at a 45° angle) to make a bias strip 4cm (1½in) wide and 1cm (³⁄₈in) longer than the head measurement to which you are making the hat.

4 Cut two peak shapes in the spotty fabric using the template on page 61 and then follow the instructions on pages 18 and 19 for making and attaching a peak, and for putting the rest of the hat together. However at step 13, ensure that the back seams match together.

5 Sew a button on each side of the hat at the point where the brim ends. When sewing the button on, pull the head ribbon down to ensure that the stitching is hidden.

6

This brown version of the Animal Hat reverses the animal and spotty fabric.

Animal Hat

Materials

- lightweight interfacing
- animal fabric, 70cm (27½in) wide x 45cm (17¾in) high to make 1 crown, 1 middle section and 1 brim
- Spotty fabric, 70 x 45cm (27½ x 17¾in) to make 1 crown, 1 middle section and 1 brim
- 2 snap fasteners
- thread

Tools

- fabric scissors
- iron
- pins
- sewing machine
- needle

1 Following the instructions on page 12, use the templates on pages 60 and 62 to cut out one crown, middle section and brim in the animal patterned fabric, and one crown, middle section and brim in the spotty fabric.

2 Using the instructions on page 13, iron the interfacing on to the patterned crown and brim and the spotty middle section.

3 To assemble the brim, follow the instructions on page 13.

4 Sew the crown and the middle section together, following the instructions on page 14.

5 Now attach the brim to the crown as on page 14, and then use the method on page 15 for making and attaching the lining.

6 Find the middle of each side of the hat. Undo the snap fastener and sew one half to the bottom of the brim and the other half to the bottom of the middle section. This enables the sides to be popped up or down and gives a cowboy look. You could also try attaching a snap fastener just to the front so that the brim can be popped back off the face.

Bicycle Hat

Materials

- ½ metre (½ yard) of bicycle fabric to make 6 triangle sections, 2 peak brims and a bias strip for the head ribbon
- spotted fabric, 50 x 35cm (19¾ x 13½in) to make 6 triangle sections for the lining
- 7.5cm (3in) length of 1cm (³⁄₈in) wide elastic
- lightweight interfacing
- heavyweight, non-iron stiff interfacing for the peak
- thread

Tools

- fabric scissors
- iron
- pins
- sewing machine

Note:

This hat has an elastic fitting at the back so you can make it in a size bigger than your child's head measurement and the elastic will pull it in to fit.

1 Use the templates on pages 60 and 61 with the directions in step 1, page 16 to cut the crown, lining, peaks and head ribbon. Follow the instructions on page 13 for using the iron-on interfacing and iron to the six bicycle-patterned triangles.

2 Follow the instructions on page 16 and 17 for making a six-part crown.

3 Follow the instructions on page 18 and 19 for making and attaching the peak, up to step 16. Here, press and fold the head ribbon under but do not stitch around the bottom of the hat at this point.

4 Fold the head ribbon back. Pin and then sew the elastic 4cm (1½in) to the side of the centre back of the hat. When securing the elastic, stitch from the bottom, straight up 2cm (¾in). Stretch the elastic across to 4cm (1½in) the other side of the centre back point and again pin and stitch in place.

5 Place the head ribbon back and, holding the fabric taut, stitch across to join the two vertical lines together.

6 Leaving out the section that contains the elastic, finish the hat by stitching 5mm (¼in) from the bottom of the crown to meet the vertical lines of stitching.

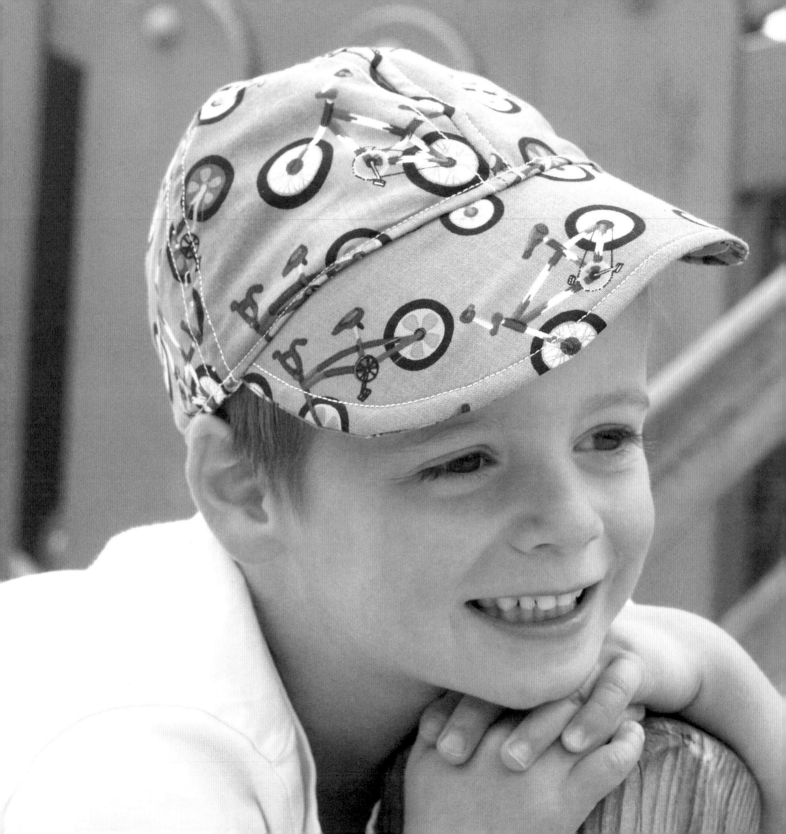

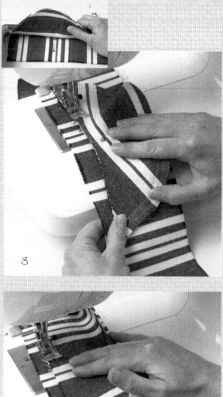

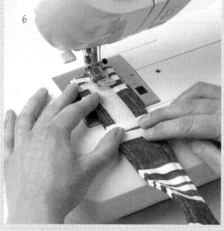

Sun Visor

Materials

- striped fabric, 70 x 35cm (27½ x 13¾in) to make 2 strips and 2 peaks
- lightweight interfacing
- 2cm (¾in) wide hook and loop tape, 8cm (3⅛in) in length
- thread

Tools

- fabric scissors
- pins
- sewing machine
- iron

1 Cut two strips of fabric (on the straight), one 65 x 9cm (25½ x 3½in) and one 65 x 7cm (25½ x 2¾in). Cut two peaks using the template on page 60. Using the instructions on page 13, iron the interfacing on to the largest strip and both peaks.

2 Place the peak pieces right sides together and pin. Sew along the outer curved edge using a 5mm (¼in) seam. Snip little triangle shapes along this edge towards the seam. Be careful not to cut through the seam line. Turn right side out and press to give a sharp edge. Top stitch 5mm (¼in) from the edge of the peak, and then add another line of stitching 5mm (¼in) above this.

3 Take the larger strip and the peak and place a pin to mark the middle of each. With the strip right side up, pin the peak 2cm (¾in) from the bottom. Stitch in place.

4 Now place the smaller strip on top of this, right side down, so that the peak is sandwiched between the strips and the tops of the strips are level. Pin in place and, starting at the end of the strip, stitch 1cm (⅜in) up from the bottom. Turn right side out and press.

5 Fold the sides and top edge neatly under by 1cm (⅜in) and press. At the ends, after you have folded and pressed, you can snip a small triangle shape off the top corners to make a neater fold. Stitch the sides and top in place.

6 Take the hook and loop tape, separate and sew on to the opposite sides of each end.

Pirate Bandana

Materials

- pirate fabric, 80 x 80cm (31½ x 31½in) to make 1 bias strip and 1 triangle
- thread

Tools

- fabric scissors
- sewing machine
- iron

1 Cut out a triangle of fabric measuring 52 x 43 x 43cm (20½ x 17 x 17in). Cut out a bias strip (cut at 45° across the fabric) 85 x 9cm (33½ x 3½in).

2 Take the triangle and use the iron to fold over a 1cm (⅜in) edge on the two shorter sides. You will need to snip off a small triangle shape on the underside of the point, to create a neat finish. Stitch along these folds to secure.

3 Take the bias strip, fold it in half lengthways, right sides together, and press. Trim the ends so that they are both at a diagonal angle. Sew along the diagonal end and continue 10cm (4in) along the strip.

4 Repeat the same process on the other side, so you are left with a gap in the middle of the band for the triangle to fit in.

5 Turn the band right side out, pushing the ends out. Fold and press the edges of the gap to match the rest of the strip. Find the centre points of the triangle and the band and pin to mark them. Matching up the pins, insert the edged triangle just inside the gap and pin in place.

6 Starting at one end, stitch along the length of the band as close to the edge as possible to hold the triangle section in place. Finally press well.

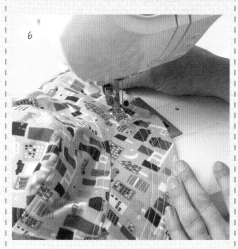

The finished hat reversed to show the spotty fabric.

Reversible Hat

Materials

- ❤ city fabric, 70 x 45cm (27½ x 17¾in) to make 1 crown, 1 middle section and 1 brim
- ❤ spotty fabric, 70 x 45cm (27½ x 17¾in) to make 1 crown, 1 middle section and 1 brim
- ❤ lightweight interfacing
- ❤ thread

Tools

- ❤ fabric scissors
- ❤ pins
- ❤ sewing machine
- ❤ iron

1 Following the instructions on page 12, use the templates on pages 60 and 62 to cut out all the pieces from the city fabric, and the same in the spotty fabric. Using the instructions on page 13, iron on the interfacing to the city patterned crown, brim and middle section.

2 Take the city patterned brim section and right sides together, sew the ends using a 5mm (¼in) seam to create a brim shape.

3 Sew the patterned crown and the middle section together by following the instructions on page 14. Now attach the single brim to the crown as on page 14.

4 Repeat the above process using the spotty fabric, so you will end up with two hat shapes. Turn the hats inside out and place one on top of the other, so they are right sides together. Ensuring that the backseams match, pin them together and, using a 5mm (¼in) seam, sew round the edge of the brims to secure the two hats together, but leave a 10cm (4in) gap towards the back of the hat.

5 Pull the hats back through the gap so that they are the right way around and push one hat up inside the other. Press the hats well to give the brim a sharp edge, and press up the edge of the gap to close it.

6 Top stitch around the brim as close to the edge as possible to close the gap in the brim. Continue with another three rows of top stitching spaced 5mm (¼in) apart.

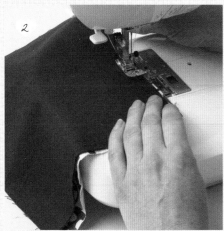

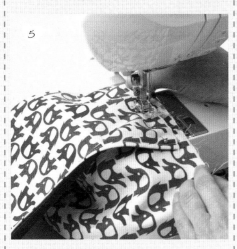

Legionnaire's Hat

Materials

- elephant fabric, 50 x 71cm (19¾ x 28in) to make 2 peaks, 4 triangles and 1 flap
- plain blue fabric, 50 x 71cm (19¾ x 28in) to make 4 triangles, 1 flap and 1 bias strip for the head ribbon
- lightweight interfacing
- heavyweight, non-iron, stiff interfacing for the brim

Tools

- fabric scissors
- pins
- sewing machine
- iron

1 Use the templates on page 60 and use the directions in step 1, page 16 to cut out two peaks in the elephant fabric, then use the crown triangle template on page 64 to cut out only four triangles in elephant fabric for the crown and four in plain blue fabric for the lining. Cut one square in each of the fabrics measuring 22 x 22cm (8¾ x 8¾in) for the flap. Take the four patterned triangles and the plain square and follow the instructions on page 13 for using the iron-on interfacing.

2 Take the two square pieces, pin them right sides together and then sew round three sides using a 5mm (¼in) seam. Trim back the seam at the corners, turn right side out and press. Top stitch 5mm (¼in) along the sides.

3 Follow the instructions on pages 16 and 17 for making a six-part crown, but join only two pieces together at a time rather than three, to create a four-part crown instead.

4 Follow the instructions on page 18 for making and attaching a peak up until step11.

5 Find the centre back points of the hat and the flap and pin to mark them. Matching these points together, pin and then sew the flap to the hat so that the patterned side will be underneath. Use a 5mm (¼in) seam.

6 Continue with the instructions on pages 18 and 19 from step 12.

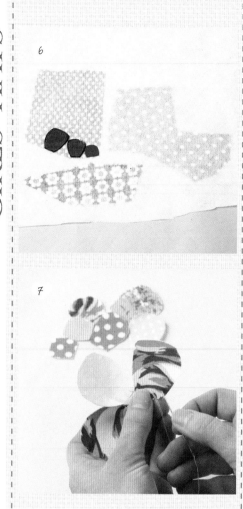

Traditional Hat

Materials

- lightweight interfacing
- floral fabric, 70 x 45cm (27½ x 17¾in) to make 1 brim, 1 middle section and 1 crown
- spotty fabric, 70 x 45cm (27½ x 17¾in) to make 1 brim, 1 middle section and 1 crown
- offcuts of fabric to make the flower petals
- thread
- button

Tools

- fabric scissors
- iron
- pins
- sewing machine
- needle

1 Following the instructions on page 12, use the templates on page 60 and 62 to cut out the pieces in the floral fabric, and the same pieces, as specified above, in the spotty fabric.

2 Using the instructions on page 13, iron the interfacing on to the patterned crown and brim and the spotty middle section. Assemble the brim following the instructions on page 13.

3 Sew the crown and the middle section together following the instructions on page 14.

4 Attach the brim to the crown as on page 14, then use the method on page 15 for making and attaching the lining.

5 Place the interfacing fusible side up and the fabric scraps on top. Using a damp cloth over the top, iron the interfacing on to the scraps.

6 Turn the interfacing over. Use the petal templates on page 63 to make a card pattern in each size. Draw round them and cut out five large, five medium and five small petals.

7 Use a running stitch along the bottom of the first large petal to pull it into a curled shape, then continue adding until all five petals are secure in a flower shape. Add a few securing stitches and then continue with the middle-sized petals on top, and then again with the smaller petals. Stitch to secure all the petals.

8 Take the button and sew it to the middle of the flower, so that all the securing stitches are hidden. Stitch the flower trim to the front of the hat.

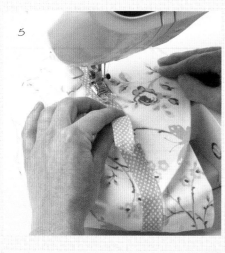

5

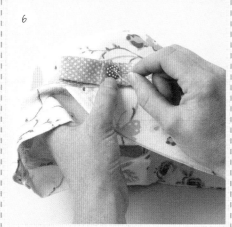

6

Bird Hat

Materials

- lightweight interfacing
- heavyweight, non-iron, stiff interfacing for the peak
- floral fabric, 70 x 80cm (27½ x 31½in) to make 1 crown, 1 middle section, 2 peaks and 1 head ribbon
- plain fabric, 70 x 30cm (27½ x 11¾in) to make 1 crown and 1 middle section
- spotty pink button
- 1 metre (1 yard) spotty ribbon
- thread

Tools

- fabric scissors
- iron
- pins
- sewing machine
- needle

1 Using the templates on page 60 and 61, cut one crown and one middle section in the floral fabric and follow the instructions on page 13 for using the iron-on interfacing on these pieces. Use the instructions on page 14 for attaching the crown to the middle section.

2 Using the plain lining fabric, cut one crown and middle section and repeat the method of attaching the crown to the middle section.

3 Cut out a head ribbon using the same plain fabric. The head ribbon should be cut on the cross (see page 16, step 1) to make a bias strip 6cm (2½in) wide and 1cm (³⁄₈in) longer than the head measurement to which you are making the hat.

4 Cut two peak shapes in the floral fabric using the template on page 64 and then follow the instructions on pages 18 and 19 for making and attaching a peak, but at step 13, make sure that the back seams match together.

5 Measure the spotty ribbon around the hat, and with the head ribbon down and out of the way, sew the spotty ribbon on to the bottom edge of the hat. Cross over the ribbon at the side of the hat where the bow will be secured.

6 Take a piece of spotty ribbon 20cm (7⅞in) long and join the ends together to form a loop. Make a smaller loop using 5cm (2in) of ribbon and slide the bigger loop through it so that it sits in the middle of the larger loop to form a bow. Stitch this to the side of the hat to hide the join, then add the button.

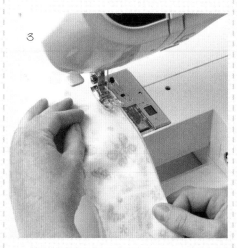

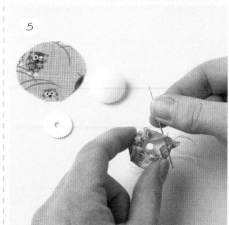

Patchwork Hat

Materials

- lightweight interfacing
- insect patterned fabric, 70 x 45cm (27½ x 17¾in) to make 1 crown, 1 brim and 1 middle section
- spotty fabric, 70 x 45cm (27½ x 17¾in) to make 2 middle sections and 1 crown
- heart-patterned fabric, 50 x 35cm (19¾ x 13¾in) to make 1 brim
- 3 x 2cm (¾in) self-covering buttons
- fabric remnants for buttons
- thread

Tools

- fabric scissors
- iron
- pins
- sewing machine
- needle

1 Following the instructions on page 12 and using the templates on pages 60 and 62, cut out one crown and one brim in the insect fabric, one crown and one middle section in the spotty fabric and one brim in the heart patterned fabric. Take the template for the middle section and use the top two-thirds to cut a section from the spotty fabric and the bottom two-thirds to cut a section from the insect fabric

2 Using the instructions on page 13, iron the interfacing on to the insect crown, heart brim and both pieces of the middle section.

3 To assemble the brim, follow the instructions on page 13. Now take the two pieces of the middle section, place them right sides together and sew them together lengthways to create one piece with the insect material at the bottom. Sew with a 2cm (¾in) seam so that the overall height of this piece is now the same as the template. Iron the seam apart and then top stitch either side of the seam. Attach the crown to the middle section following the instructions on page 14.

4 Now attach the brim to the crown as on page 14, and then use the method on pages 15 and 16 for making and attaching the lining (the lining middle section does not need to have the patchwork effect).

5 Take the fabric remnants and draw a circle on the back 1cm (⅜in) larger than the self-covering buttons. Cut this out, and then sew a running stitch around the edge of the circle. Put the button inside this circle and then pull the thread so that the fabric gathers around the button. Pull tight and stitch to secure. Place the back of the button on top and push down until it snaps. Repeat these steps for the other two buttons.

6 Neatly stitch the buttons to the front of the hat, evenly spaced.

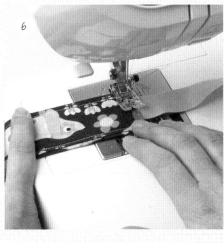

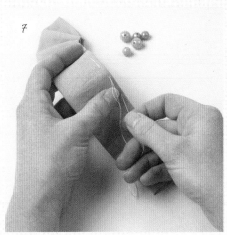

Girl's Sun Visor

Materials

- patterned fabric, 70 x 35cm (27½ x 13¾in) to make 2 strips and 2 peaks
- lightweight interfacing
- mauve grosgrain ribbon, 70cm (27½in)
- plain turquoise fabric, 25 x 10cm (9⅞ x 4in) for the flower trim
- 6 beads in different colours and sizes
- thread

Tools

- fabric scissors
- iron
- pins
- sewing machine
- needle

1 Cut two strips of the patterned fabric (on the straight), one 48 x 9cm (19 x 3½in) and one 48 x 7cm (19 x 2¾in). Cut two peaks using the peak template on page 60. Using the instructions on page 13, iron the interfacing on to the largest strip and both peaks.

2 Place the peak sections right sides together and pin. Sew along the outer curved edge using a 5mm (¼in) seam. Snip little triangle shapes along this edge towards the seam. Be careful not to cut through the seam line. Turn right side out and press to give a sharp edge. Top stitch 5mm (¼in) from the edge of the peak.

3 Take the larger strip and the peak and place a pin to mark the middle of each. With the strip right side up, pin the peak 2cm (¾in) from the bottom. Stitch in place.

4 Now place the smaller strip on top of this, right side down, so that the peak is sandwiched between the strips and the tops of the strips are level. Pin in place and starting at the end of the strip, stitch 1cm (⅜in) up from the bottom. Turn right side out and press.

5 Fold the sides and top edge neatly under by 1cm (⅜in) and press. At the ends, after you have folded and pressed, you can snip a small triangle shape off the top corners to make a neater fold. Stitch along the top of the bands but leave the ends unstitched.

6 Take the ribbon and cut two lengths 32cm (12⅝in) long. Hem and stitch one end of each ribbon. Pin the unfinished end of the ribbon inside the gap left in the patterned band and sew in place. Repeat on the other side. Now top stitch along the bottom of the band for a neat finish.

7 Take the fabric for the trim, fold it in half lengthways (right sides together) to make a tube and sew. Turn this the right way out and press the ends inside the tube. Thread a needle and sew a running stitch along the bottom of the seam edge, then pull together to make a flower shape and stitch to hold in place. Take the beads and sew to the middle of the flower so that any stitching is hidden. Sew the flower trim to the side of the sun visor.

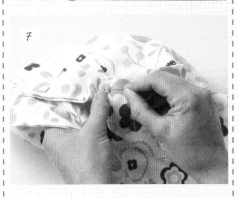

Floppy Brim

Materials

- lightweight interfacing
- floral fabric, 80 x 94cm (31½ x 37in) to make I crown, 2 brims, 1 middle section and bow trim
- spotty fabric, 70 x 30cm (27½ x 11¾in) to make 1 middle section and 1 crown
- grosgrain ribbon, 60cm (23⅝in) for head ribbon
- button
- thread

Tools

- fabric scissors
- iron
- pins
- sewing machine
- needle

1 Following the instructions on page 12, use the template on page 60 to cut out one crown and one middle section in the floral fabric. Use the templates on page 63 to cut out two brims in the floral fabric. Cut out one crown and one middle section in the spotty fabric. Using the instructions on page 13, iron the interfacing on to the floral crown, middle section and brim.

2 To assemble the brim, follow the instructions on page 13. Sew the crown and the middle section together following the instructions on page 14.

3 Now attach the brim to the crown as on page 14. Attach the lining crown and middle section together in the same way as for the hat. Place the lining section inside the hat, right way around. With the brim turned back, pin and then sew the lining to the hat, making sure that the back seams match.

4 Take the grosgrain ribbon and use the iron to stretch and curve it to a head shape for the head ribbon. Hold one section down with the iron and pull the ribbon down and through, underneath the iron. Press one end of the ribbon back by 1cm (³⁄₈in) to create a neat end.

5 Pin the head ribbon to the hat so that it covers the exposed seams. Cross over the ribbon ends at the back seam with the neat end on top, and stitch in place. Press the head ribbon up into the hat.

6 Use the bow template on page 63 to cut out two bow shapes in the floral fabric. Place right sides together and sew the bow shapes together, but leave one end open. Trim the seam at the corners, and then pull the bow through the open end so that it is the right way around. Press the bow, tuck the open end under to close the gap and overstitch to close the hole.

7 Take the bow and give it a little fold in the middle. Pin and then stitch it to the side of the hat (you will need to stitch the middle and sides of the bow to hold it in place). Finally, sew the button to the middle of the fold on the bow.

Strawberry Hat

Materials

- lightweight interfacing
- strawberry fabric, 70 x 68cm (27½ x 26½in) to make 1 brim, 1 middle section and 1 crown
- spotty fabric, 70 x 68cm (27½ x 26½in) to make 1 brim, 1 middle section and 1 crown
- spotty bias binding, 45cm (17¾in)
- strawberry bias binding, 45cm (17¾in)
- thread
- button

Tools

- fabric scissors
- iron
- pins
- sewing machine
- needle

1 Following the instructions on page 12, use the template on page 60 to cut out one crown and one middle section in the strawberry fabric and one crown and one middle section in the spotty fabric. Use the template on page 63 to cut out one brim in each of the fabrics.

2 Using the instructions on page 13, iron the interfacing on to the strawberry crown and brim and the spotty middle section. To assemble the brim, follow the instructions on page 13.

3 Sew the crown and the middle section together, following the instructions on page 14.

4 Attach the brim to the crown as on page 14, and then use the method on pages 15 and 16 for making and attaching the lining.

5 Cut each piece of bias binding into two lengths of 22cm (8¾in). Sew each piece into a loop by placing the ends together (right sides together) and machine stitching.

6 Turn the four loops right sides out and, with the seam in the middle of each loop, begin to make a flower shape by layering the ribbons on top of each other and hand sewing them together in the middle.

7 Take the button and sew it to the middle of the flower so that all the stitches are hidden. Stitch the flower trim to the side of the hat.

Daisy Hat

Materials

- daisy fabric, 50 x 75cm (19¾ x 29½in) to make 4 triangles and 2 brims
- plain fabric, 50 x 45cm (19¾ x 17¾in) to make 4 triangles for the lining
- lightweight interfacing
- green silk ribbon, 1½ metres (4ft 11in)
- thread

Tools

- fabric scissors
- iron
- pins
- sewing machine
- needle

1 Use the template on page 64 to cut four triangle shapes in the daisy fabric and four in the lining fabric. Use step 2, page 12 to help you cut two brim shapes from the template on page 64 in the daisy fabric. Take the four daisy triangles and one brim section and follow the instructions on page 13 for using the iron-on interfacing.

2 Follow the instructions on pages 16 and 17 for making a six-part crown, but instead join only two pieces together at a time to make a four-part crown.

3 Take the two brim pieces, place them right sides together and pin. Using a 5mm (¼in) seam, stitch them together, starting from the sides and then sewing along the edge of the brim. Snip small triangles into the edge of the brim; be careful not to cut the stitching. Turn the brim right side out and press well. Top stitch 5mm (¼in) along the edge of the brim.

4 Take the crown and pin the end of the brim to the back seam of the crown. Pin all round until the brim crosses over at the back. Remove the base from the sewing machine to reveal the arm and stitch the brim to the crown using a 5mm (¼in) seam.

5 For the lining crown, follow the same instructions as above but leave a 10cm (4in) gap for pulling the hat through. Make sure that the gap is left in the middle so that the top and bottom of the section are secure. Follow the instructions for attaching the lining on pages 15 and 16, from step 20.

6 Take the ribbon and neatly hand stitch it round the middle of the hat. Use a small stitch at 10cm (4in) intervals, and make sure the join is at the back of the hat.

7 Tie 65cm (25½in) of ribbon into a neat bow with ends of a similar length. Cut the ends of the ribbon at a 45° angle to give a neat finish. Stitch to the back of the hat.

Explorer's Hat

Materials

- old pair of cargo shorts
- old cotton shirt
- thread

Tools

- fabric scissors
- iron
- pins
- sewing machine

1 This hat will have the seams at each side of the hat, rather than one back seam; this is because it is more difficult with the shape of the shorts to cut each brim and middle section out in one piece. Using the templates on page 60 and 62, cut four half brims, two half middle sections and one crown from the shorts. In the shirt fabric, cut two half middle sections and a crown for the lining.

2 Take two of the brim sections and join together using a 5mm (¼in) seam to create one piece. Repeat using the other two brim sections and then follow the instructions on page 13 for putting together a brim.

3 Take the two middle sections and join them together at each side using a 5mm (¼in) seam. Now follow the instructions on page 14 for attaching the crown to the middle section.

4 Use the instructions on page 14 for putting the crown and brim together, ensuring that the side seams match.

5 Take the two lining middle sections and join together at each side using a 5mm (¼in) seam and then follow the instructions on pages 15 and 16 for attaching the lining, ensuring that the side seams match together.

6 Carefully cut out a pocket and a belt loop from the shorts, and sew to either side of the hat.

Denim Hat

Materials

- old pair of jeans
- old cotton shirt
- nautical ribbon, 58cm (23cm)
- thread

Tools

- fabric scissors
- pins
- sewing machine
- iron

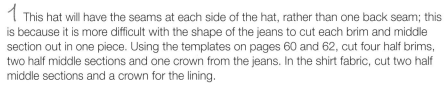

1 This hat will have the seams at each side of the hat, rather than one back seam; this is because it is more difficult with the shape of the jeans to cut each brim and middle section out in one piece. Using the templates on pages 60 and 62, cut four half brims, two half middle sections and one crown from the jeans. In the shirt fabric, cut two half middle sections and a crown for the lining.

2 Take two of the brim sections and join together using a 5mm (¼in) seam to create one piece. Repeat using the other two brim sections and then follow the instructions on page 13 for putting together a brim.

3 Take the two middle sections and join them together at each side using a 5mm (¼in) seam. Follow the instructions on page 14 for attaching the crown to the middle section.

4 Use the instructions on page 14 for putting the crown and brim together, ensuring that the side seams match together.

5 Take the two lining middle sections and join them together at each side using a 5mm (¼in) seam and then follow the instructions on pages 15 and 16 for attaching the lining, ensuring that the side seams match.

6 Take the nautical ribbon and press one end over by 1cm (³⁄₈in) to make a neat end. Pin and then machine stitch the top and bottom of the ribbon to the hat. The join for the ribbon should be at the back of the hat. Make sure that the lining of the hat is held back and taut so that the stitch line is neat inside the hat too.

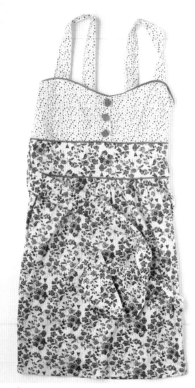

Dress Hat

Materials

- old summer dress
- lightweight interfacing
- thread

Tools

- fabric scissors
- iron
- pins
- sewing machine
- needle
- Iron

1 This hat will have the seams at each side of the hat, rather than one back seam, because the shape of the dress makes it more difficult to cut each brim and middle section out in one piece. Using the templates on pages 60 and 63, cut four half brims, four half middle sections and two crowns from the dress.

2 Using the instructions on page 13, iron the interfacing to two brim sections, two middle sections and one crown.

3 Take two of the brim sections and join together using a 5mm (¼in) seam to create one piece. Repeat using the other two brim sections and then follow the instructions on page 13 for putting together a brim.

4 Take the two middle sections and join them together at each side using a 5mm (¼in) seam. Follow the instructions on page 14 for attaching the crown to the middle section.

5 Use the instructions on page 14 for putting the crown and brim together, ensuring that the side seams match.

6 Take the two lining middle sections and join together at each side using a 5mm (¼in) seam and follow the instructions on pages 15 and 16 for attaching the lining, ensuring that the side seams match.

7 Cut the ties from the back of the dress and sew them together to create one tie 140cm (55in) long. Press well.

8 Using the template on page 62, cut four shapes to form the loops that will hold the tie in place. Place two of the loop shapes right sides together and machine sew round the edges, leaving the top open. Turn the right way around and press the open seam closed by neatly tucking the ends in, and sew to close the hole. Repeat the above to make the second loop.

9 Hand stitch the loops to the sides of the hat. Cut two buttons from the sun dress and finish by sewing a button to the bottom of each loop.

10 Thread the tie through the loops and neatly tie a bow at the back of the hat.

Templates

All the templates are shown half size unless otherwise stated. Enlarge them to 200% before use.

Middle section template

*For the hat shown in the **Basic techniques** chapter, p. 12–16, the **Animal Hat** on p. 28, **Reversible Hat** on p. 36, **Traditional Hat** on p. 40, **Patchwork Hat** on p. 44, **Floppy Brim** on p. 48, **Strawberry Hat** on p. 50, **Explorer's Hat** on p. 54, **Denim Hat** on p. 56 and **Dress Hat** on p. 58, shown in sizes 51cm (20in), 53.4cm (21in) and 56cm (22in).*

Crown template

*For the hat shown in the **Basic techniques**, p. 12–16, the **Train Hat** on p. 26, **Animal Hat** on p. 28, **Reversible Hat** on p. 36, **Traditional Hat** on p. 40, **Bird Hat** on p. 42, **Patchwork Hat** on p. 44, **Floppy Brim** on p. 48, **Strawberry Hat** on p. 50, **Explorer's Hat** on p. 54, **Denim Hat** on p. 56 and **Dress Hat** on p. 58, shown in sizes 51cm (20in), 53.4cm (21in) and 56cm (22in).*

Peak template

*For the hat shown in the **Basic techniques** section on pages 16–19, **Bicycle Hat** on p. 30, **Sun Visor** on p. 32, **Legionnaire's Hat** on p. 38 and **Girl's Sun Visor** on p. 46, shown in sizes 51cm (20in), 53.4cm (21in) and 56cm (22in).*

Crown section template

*For the **Whale Hat** on p. 20, shown in sizes 43cm (17in), 45.7cm (18in) and 48.2cm (19in).*

Middle section template

*For the for **Bow Hat** on p. 22, shown in sizes 43cm (17in), 45.7cm (18in) and 48.2cm (19in).*

Crown triangle template

*For the hat shown in the **Basic techniques** section on pages 16–19 and the **Bicycle Hat** on p. 30, shown in sizes 51cm (20in), 53.4cm (21in) and 56cm (22in).*

Middle section template

*For the **Train Hat** on p. 26 and the **Bird Hat** on p. 42, shown in sizes 51cm (20in), 53.4cm (21in) and 56cm (22in).*

Peak template

*For the **Train Hat** on p. 26.*

Crown template

*For the **Bow Hat** on p. 22, shown in sizes 43cm (17in), 45.7cm (18in) and 48.2cm (19in).*

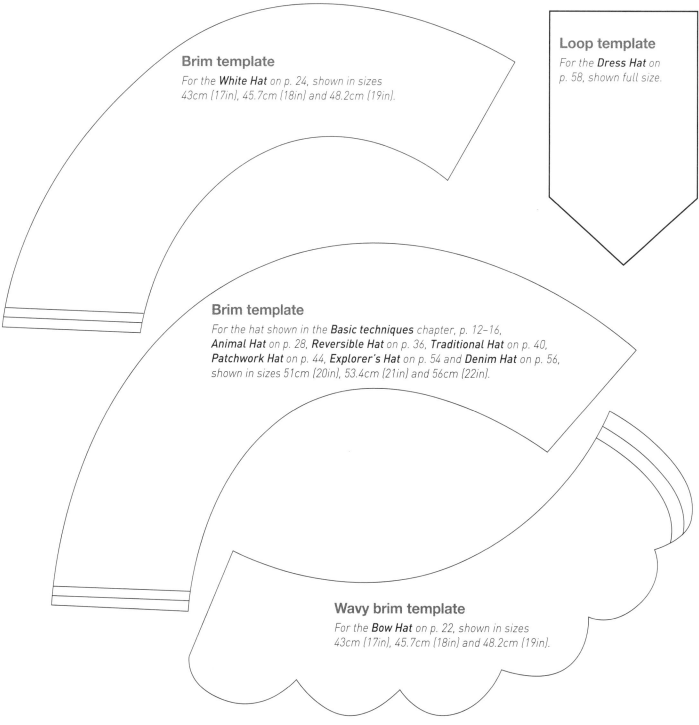

Brim template

*For the **White Hat** on p. 24, shown in sizes
43cm (17in), 45.7cm (18in) and 48.2cm (19in).*

Loop template

*For the **Dress Hat** on
p. 58, shown full size.*

Brim template

*For the hat shown in the **Basic techniques** chapter, p. 12–16,
Animal Hat on p. 28, **Reversible Hat** on p. 36, **Traditional Hat** on p. 40,
Patchwork Hat on p. 44, **Explorer's Hat** on p. 54 and **Denim Hat** on p. 56,
shown in sizes 51cm (20in), 53.4cm (21in) and 56cm (22in).*

Wavy brim template

*For the **Bow Hat** on p. 22, shown in sizes
43cm (17in), 45.7cm (18in) and 48.2cm (19in).*

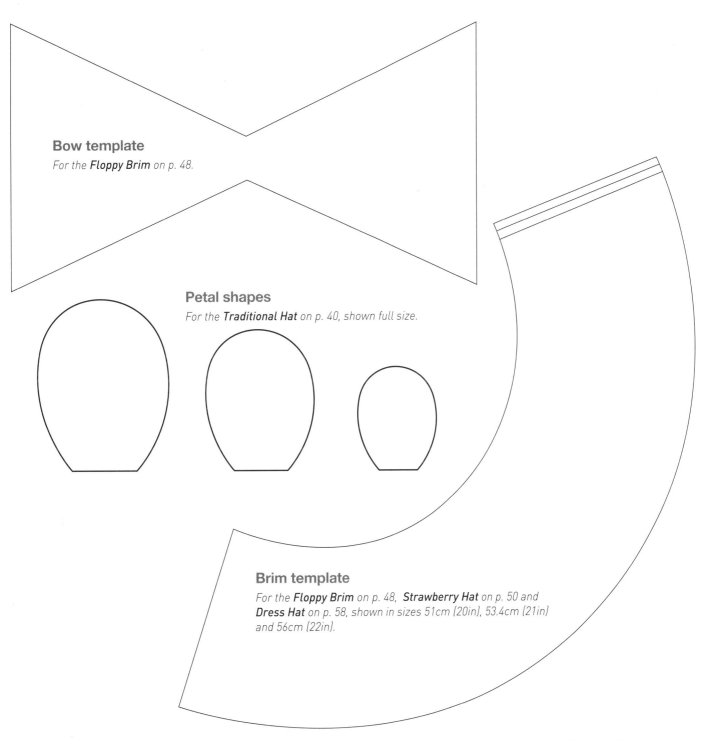

Bow template

*For the **Floppy Brim** on p. 48.*

Petal shapes

*For the **Traditional Hat** on p. 40, shown full size.*

Brim template

*For the **Floppy Brim** on p. 48, **Strawberry Hat** on p. 50 and **Dress Hat** on p. 58, shown in sizes 51cm (20in), 53.4cm (21in) and 56cm (22in).*

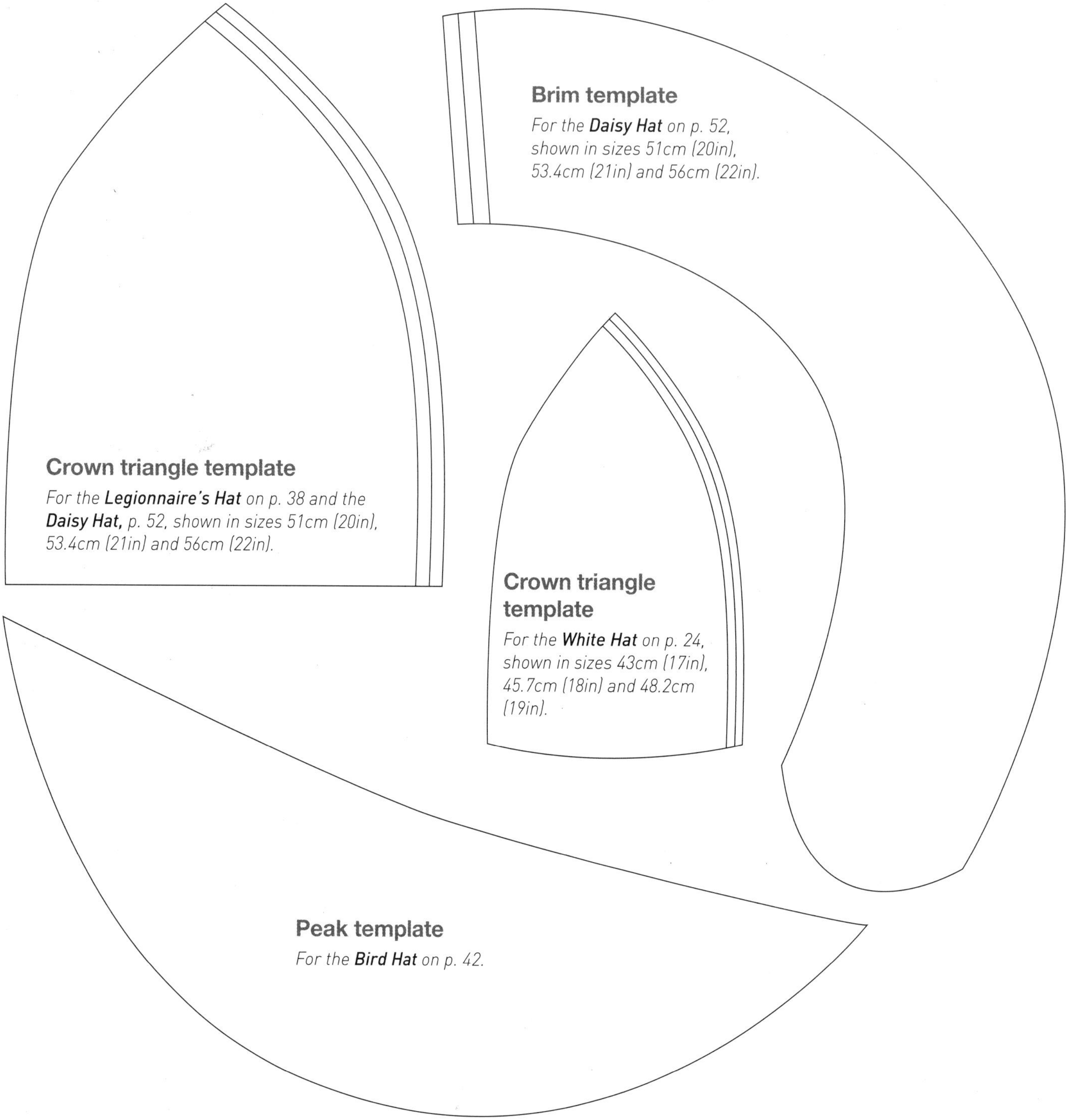

Brim template

*For the **Daisy Hat** on p. 52,
shown in sizes 51cm (20in),
53.4cm (21in) and 56cm (22in).*

Crown triangle template

*For the **Legionnaire's Hat** on p. 38 and the
Daisy Hat, p. 52, shown in sizes 51cm (20in),
53.4cm (21in) and 56cm (22in).*

**Crown triangle
template**

*For the **White Hat** on p. 24,
shown in sizes 43cm (17in),
45.7cm (18in) and 48.2cm
(19in).*

Peak template

*For the **Bird Hat** on p. 42.*